¡VEO VEO!

VEO VEO

NÚMEROS

MARIE ROESSER

TRADUCIDO POR
DIANA OSORIO

Gareth Stevens
PUBLISHING

conceptos
básicos

¡Veo números!

3

Veo 1 mascota.

Veo 2 guitarras.

Veo 3 pollitos.

Veo 4 pastelitos.

Veo 5 libros.

13

Veo 6 dulces.

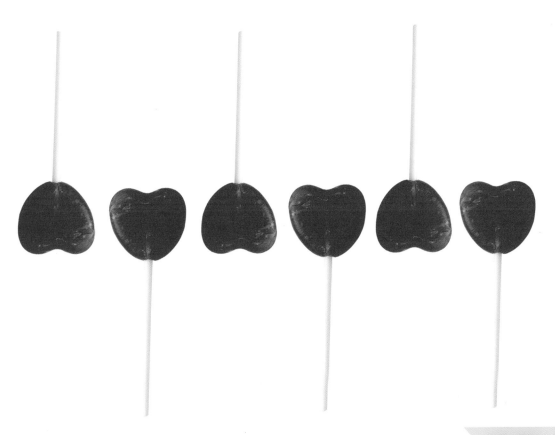

Veo 7 lápices
de colores.

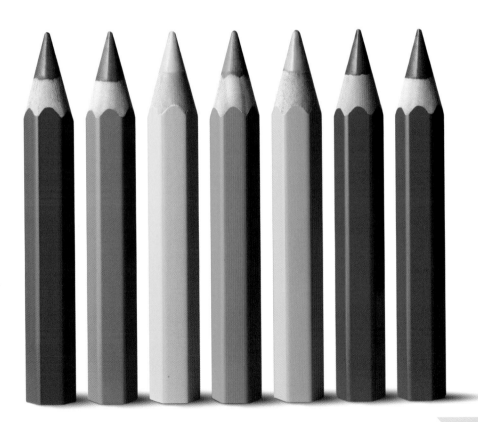

Veo 8 juguetes.

Veo 9 hormigas.

¡Veo 10 fresas!

23

Please visit our website, www.garethstevens.com. For a free color catalog of all our high-quality books, call toll free 1-800-542-2595 or fax 1-877-542-2596.

Library of Congress Cataloging-in-Publication Data
Names: Roesser, Marie, author.
Title: Veo veo números / Marie Roesser.
Description: New York : Gareth Stevens Publishing, 2022. | Series: ¡Veo veo!
 | Includes index.
Identifiers: LCCN 2020013409 | ISBN 9781538267950 (library binding) | ISBN
 9781538267936 (paperback) | ISBN 9781538267943 (6 Pack)| ISBN 9781538267967
 (ebook)
Subjects: LCSH: Number concept–Juvenile literature. | Counting–Juvenile
 literature. | Reading–Juvenile literature.
Classification: LCC QA141.15 .R64 2022 | DDC 513.5–dc23
LC record available at https://lccn.loc.gov/2020013409

First Edition

Published in 2022 by
Gareth Stevens Publishing
111 East 14th Street, Suite 349
New York, NY 10003

Translator: Diana Osorio
Editor, Spanish: Rossana Zúñiga
Designer: Katelyn E. Reynolds
Editor: Rossana Zúñiga

Photo credits: Cover, p. 1 Pingun/Shutterstock.com; cover, back cover, p. 1 (blue background) Irina Adamovich/
Shutterstock.com; p. 3 Isabel Pavia/Moment/Getty Images; p. 5 GlobalP/iStock/Getty Images Plus; p. 7 Pavel
Vorobyev /EyeEm/Getty Images; p. 9 Liliboas/E+/Getty Images; p. 11 tbd/ iStock/Getty Images Plus; p. 13
aluxum/iStock/Getty Images Plus; p. 15 EvgeniiAnd/iStock/Getty Images Plus; p. 17 malerapaso/iStock/Getty
Images Plus; p. 19 Taya Gokita/EyeEm/Getty Images; p. 21 arlindo71/E+/Getty Images; p. 23 pixitive/E+/
Getty Images.

Printed in the United States of America

Some of the images in this book illustrate individuals who are models. The depictions do not imply actual
situations or events.

CPSIA compliance information: Batch #CWGS22: For further information contact Gareth Stevens, New York, New York at 1-800-542-2595.

Find us on